From Inside These Wild Ones

Poems

Ryan Van Lenning

Book 3 in the *Re-Membering* Series

Copyright © 2025
by Wild Nature Heart Press

All rights reserved.
Use of this material with attribution is welcome.

For inquires, contact
ryan@wildnatureheart.com

Cover Design by author

ISBN: 978-1-7368776-9-2

WildNatureHeart.com

Books By the Author

In the Re-Membering Series:

Re-Membering
One Bright and Real Caress
From Inside These Wild Ones

Trust the Ceremony, F*ck the Ceremony,
Trust the Ceremony

Forthcoming:

Becoming Beautiful Barbarians
An Ambitious Silence
Riverever
Within the Cave Something Pulses

"All relationships are transformations that leave both me and the world changed by one another. Encounters in which one penetrates the other and leaves it altogether different than it was before. Everything changes when we engage with it in emotional contact. No encounter leaves us the same. We cannot be neutral.
We are always already swept up."

—Andreas Weber, Matter & Desire: An Erotic Ecology

"Owning up to being an animal, a creature of earth. Tuning our animal senses to the sensible terrain: blending our skin with the rain-rippled surface of rivers, mingling our ears with the thunder and the thrumming of frogs, and our eyes with the molten gray sky. Feeling the polyrhythmic pulse of this place -- this huge windswept body of water and stone. This vexed being in whose flesh we're entangled.

Becoming earth. Becoming animal.
Becoming, in this manner, fully human."

—David Abram, Becoming Animal: An Earthly Cosmology

CONTENTS

INTRODUCTION 1
WE HAD OUR HABITS 4
    Soft in Bending Unflagging Song 5
    The Silent Here of Things 6
    My Paws Are Alive 7
    Apprenticeship 8
    Words in This Forest 9
    All in the Same House 10
    I Had My Habits 11
    A Lunatic Colossal 13
    I Have Been Known to Bark 14
    Pulsed and Awed 15
    Gorgeous Storm 16
    First Meeting 17
    Last Glimpse of May 19
    Wink You Into That Obsidian Night 21
DEEP WE (EARTH INTIMACIES) 22
    We Are 23
    The Dream Was In the Beast of Me 25
    And Love Is a Tree Is a Human Is 26
    Ash Kin 27
    Naked As a Rotting Log 29
    Riverever 31
    Earth Intimacies 33
    The Moon Is a Turtle Is a Human Heart 35
    From Inside These Wild Ones 37
    What Do You Hear When You Listen to Lichen Grow? 39
    Wild Syllable of Trust on My Lips 40
    Kissing Other-Kin In the Center of My Cells 41
    Activating Metabolism, Acquired and Acrobatic 43

We Are the Monarch Who Finds A Way 46
ACROBATIC EXPERIMENTS IN WETNESS 48
  Your Body and the Bear's Growl 49
  Kiss Me a Blackberry 51
  A Sacred Bee Perhaps 53
  Wet 55
  Wild Well of Need Well Met 57
  Bryosensual 58
  Oh Nom Nom 59
  Mystery of Red 60
  Secret Mandala 61
  Wild Rose Hips 63
BEAUTIFUL BEASTS AT THE CROSSROADS 65
  Beautiful Beast at the Crossroads 66
  The Deeper We Crawl, The Brighter We Burn 68
  Suddenly, I Was a Bear 69
  Autumn Otters 71
  Scribbling Newt Bellies 73
  Sea Lion Soul 74
  Thank You, Bear, Devour Me 75
DEEP BELONGING 77
  My Name is Belonging... 78
  Spiral-In-Beauty Way... 80
  That Which Will Not Be Tamed 81
  Arrhythmia 83
  Citizen of Her Flow 84
  In This Deep 85
  All the Way Down 86
  What I Meant... 87
  In That Old Country 88
  How Many Leaves Have Landed In Me? 89

ALL THE STONES IN US ARE BIRDS 90
    All the Stones In Us Are Birds 91
    Thrush's Answer 93
    Owl 94
    Wild Wings of Mourning 95
    Bright and Awe-full Symphony of Things 98
    Show At the Edge of the Meadow 99
    No Longer Here 101
    Did You Grow a New Bird, Forest? 102

PERMISSION 103
    First Permission 104
    Catkins Can, Can You? 106
    Trust, Beaver 107
    Password 108
    When That Hard Marble Hits You 109
    Not Different Than 110
    Cut One From The Mystery 112
    Caldera: Sacred Well 113
    Madrone Skin 115
    Leaving the Grass 116
    What Song-Basket Could Contain It All? 117
    Loyal to Earth 119

About the Author 121
About Wild Nature Heart 122
Other Titles in the *Re-Membering* Series 123
Excerpts From Ryan's Upcoming Books 126

INTRODUCTION

Some years ago, I launched an experiment: for most of a couple years, I lived almost entirely outside in local forests. Either with a tent or without, with only the breathing sky as heart-home roof, I called redwoods and rivers my home, my kin.

As the poem 'The Silent Here of Things' puts it: "I never walked so slow, never inhaled so many trees / savored so many stars / Dawn hung around my neck / like a sigil / river stones became emblems / of radiant belonging."

Sometimes I would nudge into morning breakfast with swallows, mallards, deer, silver lupine, and the poet William Stafford on the riverbank. Other days were met with the scent of bay tree and bear, peregrine and the treasures of storms.

All this was by choice, a decision I made in order to live closer to the land, learn from the seasons, and align with my purposes. I wanted to lean into a multi-species, embodied, and soulful participation in the unfolding symphony of life. It was simultaneously one of the most grounding and exhilarating couple years in my life. It was not always easy, but never have I felt so consistently alive.

But truth be told, it was also a feeble attempt to escape—or at least not overly invest in—the values and conceits of Modernity, and its accumulated noise, machines, waste, and wars. While the story of that wrestling match is a different one, I can say that it provided me with both the perspectives and fuel to be able to stay rooted while also staying with The Trouble.

When I crossed the threshold of that pilgrimage, I had said I was apprenticing to the seasons and deep listening. To the call of poetry and guiding people into their own versions of deeper belonging in their own lives. The lessons and insights are incalculable, ones I am still integrating.

I learned everything is a window. I learned Everywho speaks and is unabashedly themselves. I learned a keener inter-dependence with the living and dying more-than-human world. I learned to caress the contours of a Grand Meandering pouring mountain hearsay into the ears of the sea.

Above all (below all?), I learned that whatever deep belonging is, it is something not earned, but inherent, by virtue of our intimate relationships within the animate web of life, as citizen of the Cosmos. There can be no loneliness in such a robust community.

All these are lessons and messages that can be difficult to hear within the stale scripts of an OverCulture that we inherited, one that has severed us from so much that is our human birthright.

This experiment in threshold living was the context in which the poems in the first books *Re-Membering, High-Cooing Through the Seasons, and One Bright and Real Caress* were born, as well as the majority of the poems found here.

An anarchist ecology would remind us that we've only been inside this rusty cage of the OverCulture for a few seconds and here as humans for a few minutes, from the perspective of Deep Time.

Most of those minutes have not been cursed with the burden of over-civilization. Yet we've been here as Earth and Cosmos for billions—this 'We' is infinitely more entangled than we generally appreciated.

As 'We Are' puts it: The Era of I-Over is over. *Deep We is calling.*

The miracle is: we can always still lean into the raucous conversion of a world abuzz with vitalities. We can invoke our stardust and mycelium citizenships into threshold experiments. The biopoetics of fungi and watershed intimacies, of esoteric amphibianism and whimsical time-banditry with tree people suggest ways to not only join with coyotes stalking the perimeter of chronically-successful/gloriously-failed empires, but playfully put down paw prints into the dirt of a post-imperial butterfly earth.

In the end, my hope is that *From Inside These Wild Ones* can be a call to re-member and rejoin the animate web of life—welcoming mystery, longing, intimacy, and sensual delight as integral to belonging on/with/as Earth, perhaps sparking new apprenticeships along the way.

These are dispatches from somewhere in that Entanglement.

WE HAD OUR HABITS

Soft in Bending Unflagging Song

That we chose the well-brambled life
Or it chose us when we untamed

That we lived a well-warbled life
Or it lived through us just the same

But there was a time when we knew not
Moon nor River by their names

And there was an era when ears were dim
no trills and chirps amidst the din

A time forlorn with all the dams
at every slightly hurdled rock

when feet and heart were weary weak
and all our paths and trails blocked

But then we ate the mountains whole
or they ate us when once we walked

That then we heard the rivers' flow
Soft in bending unflagging song

That then we sipped the heron slow
Fished in water for silence deep

And cast our line in patient art
to catch the things for us to keep

The Silent Here of Things

I finally stood in the lush truth of it.

I never walked so slow, never inhaled
so many trees
savored so many stars.

Dawn hung around my neck
like a sigil
river stones became emblems
of radiant belonging.

Some 'I' in me had said, I can't live
like this

but some big eye in me—
I think it was an owl—replied, Yes.

Yes you can.

They just kept letting me in.

Everywhere I didn't knock.
No keys. No doors.

The living sky my heart-home roof.

Only the silent here of things
on the back of the map

where all the real places are.

My Paws Are Alive

Don't ask me why River and her tributaries
converged in me

pouring mountain hearsay
into the ears of my sea

Don't beg the reasons a bear
roamed into the den of my corrugated heart
taking turns hunting and hibernating
through the wildlands within

Why a Sitka spruce sat up straight
in my soul or a Nutcracker turned up
in my whirling blood
squirreling secrets away
as snacks for a winter minute
is not for humans to discover

It is enough to know
my paws are alive

My tongue arrives
at the wonder of things

spilling out like fresh meadows
after the storm

Apprenticeship

To live among the hucklebush
with ferns and forest ever-lush
to learn to sing from hermit thrush
the slugs they teach so slow

The froggy croaks they keep me cracked
The crawling oaks they coax me back
These nightly cloaks they stroke my back
the moon she taught me whole

I'd hunted, hoarded all life long
but not the things that held my song
Nor the things that made me strong
They sure did take their toll

Now hunting has a different aim
The gatherings a different game
The tools I use have different names
within this chest and soul

So still I watch the heron's hunt
and listen to the river's run
apprenticed to the earth and sun
These lovers taught me Flow

Words in This Forest

There are words in this forest
older than your grandfather

older than the grandmother tree
on his farm

Words even older than the soil
holding her up

since before
she was a seed

They're entangled together here
forming silent songs

called root and flow
called change and be
called here and now.

You can't pronounce them with your tongue.

All in the Same House

I will do my best not to bring Sun and Moon
into this yet again.

It's just that when you all live in the same house
things get cozy

They're always just there—
when you open your eyes with Jay
and close your eyes with Owl

Every conversation is about the Eco
whether or not there is any weather

I invite friends over for lunch
a jam session, a glass of river

but it's too hot to eat and they get a glimpse
of the way turkey feathers spark up
in the valley glow

while the bathroom habits of great blue herons
become all too familiar

We all begin speaking not unlike ducks do
noticing how even jackrabbits lounge around
in the living room heat

So we wait until Sun
makes some excuse to leave—

we can finally shake off our lethargy
to play at something real
making every star a meal

I Had My Habits

It's not something one speaks about publicly.

Did I go wild in the woods
or find merely a measure of meaning
sharp as a storm?

Yet I recall growing dawns on me like leaves
riotous rivers running through me

Something exquisite becoming green
in the body.

Oh, I could dance and dance
and never reach the bottom.

The world was a ladybug, a lichen left to be.

All was rainbow, Everything
a universe

the poison oak, a guardian
and ox-eyed daisies lazy free
the autumn sky, abundant muddy me.

I had my habits—
Living on my in-and-out breath

Under a mushroom
Over a bough, bowed with moss.

Seasons saw me.

I drew a few to my hearth
Foxes from their hidden dens
Bears from hibernation
Falcons from their perches

Feral ones fleeing cages.

Conversations with the least of them,
the most of them.

I had no scrap of saddle
No undue doing
No yoke of note
but their sweetest voice.

Dropped my dreaming stone in the creek
and fleshed it out so still.

Still...What 'I' opened?

What eyes opened!

A Lunatic Colossal

Floating in the east,
All dithery and blossomed

Apluckered light in flantic whole
A lunatic colossal

        (more round about than Chaucer)

Grandly goosed in gibbous garb
Her gosling eye so shone

Coy as cat and slicker yet
She yearned her lover home

        (she learned her lover's poem)

So in the West in full-boned ease
All gandery and glistened

Reclining brithe and skinkery
Quite clueless but alistenin':

An ursine man with plinket eyes
Skin-gathered and complete

Came glatherin' in the sky
All free of boot and sweet

I Have Been Known to Bark

I admit I've been known to bark
loud and unrestrained,
like a sea-lion or a bear
when no one is around to leer, or hear

or twitter too, like killdeer do
when they're settling in for you

But not the heron's croaking lark
for that I judge him much too harsh
despite the wisdom in his eyes
I find I'm not the croaking type

But many tunes, I dare declare
I'll cry alone and sad
at the ways of a wicked world
the latest rage or fad

But also in a startled joy
of beauty so alive
laughing's not so far behind
when warblers sing and otters dive

The impossibility of it all
like spring from winter and summer's fall
Or feathers flown as seeds are sown
And back to shore to find what grows

Babble and skat out loud to hear
echoes over water near
bouncing off the cliff so stark:
Yes, I've been known to bark

Pulsed and Awed

What do you do when above all
It's the rhythm uncooked,
the rush of the raw

A moon-kissed river within and thawed
Most precious, unbolted and brightly awed
Original blood pulsed and odd?

When even if you owned nothing at all
Nothing else under silvered skies
But the sink of the sun, the startling rise

When the push and pull of the thing was the all?

And the goldupongold, the unlikely prize
wealth beyond dreams deferred or dried

not festered or stunk or sunk with a load
but light as a feather, finely floating
like a film on the water finally flowing?

What do you do but swim and ride
waggling and wagging and wild-eyed?

Gorgeous Storm

This gorgeous storm
keeps getting stuck in my teeth

as if I could bite-size my way
to destiny

when all I want is to have it come
racing out my lungs

like a waterfall plunging
over my luscious tongue

flooding all the landscapes
of my crooked life

to join the wrens and warblers
and beloved lusts

of a wounded world
washing away the old debris

Please, Storm, please, knock down
the weak branches of my being

Prune me for the season
I am meant to live

First Meeting

First meeting with my new land mates.

The purpose was to get to know each other
and discuss respective chores.

In attendance: rabbit, deer, quail, fern, peregrine, bay
laurel, redwood, madrone, spider, squirrel, oak, snake,
thistle, poison oak, wind, beetle, and walnut.

Fox came late, as usual.
Then kept leaving and coming back.

Absent: Owl, possum, raccoon, bat.
(being nocturnal, they have a tough time
with morning meetings).

I hope they'll read the minutes.

Turns out Moon was present the whole time,
but we didn't see her–
she had her new coat on.

We opened with an ice breaker:
What's your favorite thing about autumn?
What's the silliest thing you've done this year?

Madrone said she stripped for the deer folk.
You can guess squirrel's favorite thing.

Wind said this meeting was the silliest thing,
and left the meeting early,
knocking nuts off Walnut and Laurel in the process.

Wrapping up, we reached a decision by consensus:

We will each be ourselves and allow the other
to be themselves.

This is by far the largest home I've lived in
and by far the most housemates I've ever had.

So many that I haven't yet met them all.

But I hope to get to know them intimately
as the seasons unfold.

Last Glimpse of May

Sandflies are silent but persistent
wanting something on the inside
of my skull

Fortunately, I have legs
that give me a slight height advantage
and a spine that pivots my head
towards Venus in the heart of Gemini
already gazing searchingly at me
inches above Sunday's goodbye.

Sand is no less a bed
for not having cost a month's salary
at that store people love to talk about
and Willows no less a backyard
for not owning it

big hard rocks are great
for building houses
but little, soft rocks are better
for sleeping on

It has the built-in feature
of containing ancient crystals
the color of nautical dusk
and blue glass
and I swear a little bit o' Mars

who is even hotter
than fire season in the Central Valley

but that doesn't prevent crickets
and plovers from swapping bedtime stories

or from crying onomatopoeically
for their version of what happened

and while River spills her guts out
into and out of the arms of Evening Star

a satellite and a jackrabbit slide by–
a last glimpse of May.

Wink You Into That Obsidian Night

Frogs announce it's bath-time,
but Time and Space are just bad habits
when you take off your robe
to dip into the cosmic hot springs

Ease your wrinkled mind
and wash off all that debris
that's collected around your eyes and ears
since Sun cracked itself open this morning

when you were just a baby
so innocent and bright-eyed
and full of fear and dreams

Settle in for a bedtime story–
Which is it this time,
the one about the trickster thief
who saved the world

or the one about the drunken saint
who cracked open a thousand hearts?

Sand and Moon quibble
over who loves you more
and owl and coyote take turns
tucking you in with their lullabies–
winking you into that obsidian night

where threads of dreamcloth weave themselves
around your hungry heart

Until once again you awake a newborn
Tossing fresh songs into liberation sky

DEEP WE (EARTH INTIMACIES)

We Are

"I pledge allegiance. I pledge allegiance to the soil of Turtle Island, and to the beings who thereon dwell one ecosystem in diversity under the sun. With joyful interpenetration for all." - From Gary Snyder's 'For All'

The Era of I-Over is over. *Deep We* is calling.

Like you, I was assigned only human at birth—a severe abbreviation, to say the least.

Too many 'not-mes' in me to remain an 'I', I surrender to the immense We. This is me coming out/in as We.

Vast skies and deep soil live within—bacteria and bears, colors and con-fusions.

Disturbingly, (in the best sense of that word), Elder Fire and Ash Kin pierced me with questions I have no right to refuse. The midnight cries of the remains of those who didn't survive flow through our nervous system, wiggling us towards liberatory futures. Though we try, we cannot flee our entanglement. The symphonies of howling disguise themselves as itching until we listen and accept them, offering refuge in our body-hearts.

There's no going back.

Prior to that—a kiss from, an indictment by, an apprenticeship to bear. It was from bear I learned to eat everything, to be with everything. I learned that if I didn't learn how to embody the truths dancing inside, I would be destroyed—confirming the wisdom of Gnostic Thomas, "If you bring forth what is within you, what you bring forth will save you. If you do not bring forth what is within you, what you do not bring forth will destroy you."

Along the way rainbow eagle flew into our chest, tattooing the shape of sky in us.

Dung beetle-dug in, turtle-moon paced slowly through our veins. Hermit thrush threw ever-widening iridescent loops.

Then Riverever forever foriver. I was done for. We were born and are always being born. A cascade of unfolding co-becomings, erotic and eclectic.

The Era of I-Over is over. Deep We is calling.

Calling for a collaboration to compost the dead and dying body of the over-culture, decolonizing hearts, dismantling identity-prisons that have us all by the throats.

Impossibilities are emerging, as common as ants.

Not just beyond the binary, but beyond the non-binary. Gender- and human-expansive. Trans-species, polyphyletic, shapeshifting, micro-animist, archetypally-curious, oneirogenic (dream producing), rhizomatic, symbiotic, omnivorous and cosmic-fluid.

We are unmuzzling the beasts within. We are With-nessing something new. We are pulsating raw and riddled rhythms into the ecosystem of robust nows.

We are.

The Dream Was In the Beast of Me

The dream was in the beast of me
before I woke the yoke.

The egg was in the dream of me
before I broke the yolk.

The yolk in me was rich and free
before the scaly shine.

The fish was in the bear in me
before I cast my line.

The bear was in the cave of me
before the ocean's spell.

The crab was in the sea of me
before I cracked the shell.

And Love Is a Tree Is a Human Is

The idea of what a Tree is
is hugely variable
Is not different
than an idea of what
a Human is. A Human Is
a creature that creates
is a being that emotes
that aesthetes, that prosthetes,
that secretes secret worlds
part mammal, part microbial mama,
part plant, part star
part purr, part roar
part silent looking up yonder
part soaking up water under
What a Human is a Tree is
a promise is a possibility is
permeable to clouds
and Love is something
Humans and Trees exchange
and Love is a Tree is a Human
is something
the idea of which
Is highly variable

Ash Kin

Waking up at 2am
covered in the remains
of those that didn't survive

This is called deep intimacy
with the world

A blanket of kin-fir and kin-grass
kin-beetle and kin-deer

A deep breath of kin-bear and kin-pine
that could not escape

And haven't we all now passed through
the portal
into the Era of No Escape?

Some say there's wisdom in that,
but there's a pain in our
(Fill-in-the-blank)

Everything is streaming now—
Amazon's Prime and Amazon fires
Netflix and networks of mycelium
YouTube and Metoo
Disease and Dis-ease

There's a rumor going around
that what used to be called rivers
in the old tongue

will be replaced by streams
of discarded iPhones
and micro-plastics

But We, believers in wild water,
still go by the old indicators—

Salmon spawning
and storms of truth

Dark topsoil
and the luminous humus of heart

Depth of connection
And degrees of presence

Because Earth too
is transmitting non-stop
through us—and we want to inhabit
the green zone.

We all are in each other now—
and isn't this what the elders
have been saying the whole time?

Naked As a Rotting Log

We're debris that's breaking down
And building up the wild woods

We're naked as a rotting log
No things to prove or shoulds

We're a thousand broken twigs
That no one will ever see

We're a croaking raven raving mad
Atop the Doug fir tree

We're the shadow of the season
Casting ever shorter days

We're the fern that frees itself
And the spores that float away

We're the wound that slowly heals
With the bending balm of time

We're that would that would its could
If could could find its rhyme

We're the spider building webs
Too light for eyes to catch

We're the bird that flings its songs
To urge its eggs to hatch

We're the mud upon the feet
That brings the wisdom down

We're the duff as thick as hearts
The root that dives the ground

We're the lichen laying layers
Over eons in the wind

We're the prayer in vernal air
On which all the things depend

We're the slug sweet as can be
The warbler warmth that morning sings

We're the countless needles knowing
Where to fall and seek the slowing

And the earth who's always turning
Round the sun who's always burning

We're the beast, the belly, and the biting
The bone and bile, whim and wilding

The untold truth and whole damn show
We're the poem that overflows.

Riverever

(for E.E. Cummings)

River stone sun moon
let by let, in day dream swoon

he sang his yes and flung his no
flow by flow, stone by stone

thereby came his riverever
(so riverly and thus forever)

get by get, let getting set
by piece and piece and picking up
the dustly dust that had been down

moon river stone sun
(yet he's not the only one)

wave by wet, bird by wing
bee and sting, trees so ringed
not faraway, but nearby far
into dreaming breathe big star
one by one, not two by two
how he wonders, do you too?

pebbles down or time it pins ya
empty pockets 'til it getchya

but then and now and oftening
past did its went and forgotten things

all 'I'll nevers' said, and 'i'll bes'
but all the things in between,
oh the things…

so sun moon river stone
(yet they're not the only one)

flesh by flesh, touch by touch
bark by skin by scale as much
dream one wakes, wide by wind
wild it, yes, remembering

he on cheek them, kisses, winks it
whenever floats it up, then sinks it

Earth Intimacies

You act surprised when Grandfather Grasshopper
flies into your ears

But know you have a duty to send your ears out
hopping across the land

Chomping on the big and little
and allying with Wind

You'll be forgiven for thinking
you know who Wind is,
some dull breeze or background

When Wind is the wing-lift
of every sky-bound being

Is pheromones, pollen
ash kin and Ever-born,
bearer of unconventional truths.

Sex and death and wisdom
in conversation with one another.

Just as Rain isn't always grief
and Thunder isn't always anger

But ways to communicate intimacy
with what is.

When Grasshopper flies into your mouth
You don't know what to say

So you say it
with a strange and dusty accent

Just as Water speaks a thousand dialects
in their undying pilgrimage

So when Grasshopper flies into your heart
their green gears grin
at all your precious purities.

When you find yourself
no longer fearing
the depths of entanglement

You become gloriously impure,
a porous prism pulsating.

Your presence, an homage
Your feeling, a spell

Making the world anew
in each moment

The Moon Is a Turtle Is a Human Heart

The moon is a turtle—
how have you not known before?

How she carries her home across
the parched land one step at a time

a reservoir of soothing elixirs
in her silver belly

for the people on the edge
for the people burning at both ends
for the people fearful of their own wholeness

For you—you who are on the cusp
of tremendous things.

For she has drunk deeply
from the world
and knows how to survive the season—
how have you not understood this before?

How with her Moon-eye-point-of-view
and her pace with peace poured into it
she is not rattled by the noise
that reigns below—
how have you not noticed before?

How she buries her song egg
in the sand of the sky

always hatching new songs
and intoning the old prayers

of love and change

of light and dark.

How have you not heard them
like this before?

How she carves a bright life in you
always coming and going—
you can't make of her a bride to keep in your house
as an ornament
but you must be the bridemoon yourself.

When the moment of cracking arrives
and the sound is a marvel
heard by all the lovers out there
who have their faces turned
towards the big sky.

You are one of them.

You are one of the great lunatic lovers
with one ear pitched on the horizon
the other turned within the deep well.

And you discover the cracking never stops.

That it is the cracking that draws
the beautiful patterns all over your shell
that you buried in the sand of the sky.

You discover that the moon is a turtle
and you are the moon—
how have you not known this before?

From Inside These Wild Ones

I'd apologize
but that isn't what bears do

For a summer day my fists turned into paws—
that anyone could understand

But if it were only a day
then why now does my snout
draw itself towards the winter cave
sitting on a canyon hip like a tea cup
about to pour itself
into my hibernating belly?

Why does fur blanket my body
like an old-growth forest?

Why does the scent of a woman
half-mile down canyon
enter me like a sword of truth?

That turtle in me is slow and steady
because I'm already where I'm at

I carry my home and the weight is significant
yet no matter how fast your rabbit-mind,
it will not catch up with my tortoise soul

it'll have you running circles around yourself
like the great task of Sisyphus

I'd attempt an explanation,
but my words come out as chirps and squawks,
even bright whistles at dawn

So many birds have landed in me
I fear my tongue is tied

I can't feel my arms without clutching
a claw full of feathers, the color of trust

The fear in you perhaps belongs to the wren in me
but I won't let that stop the eagle in me
from hunting you

Or the worm in me from hinting to you
how I've dug in your soil and turned you over

how I compost even your darkest shit
and bring up blooms from it all

You can thank me later
once you've managed to blink me out
of your terrible night-time vision

Give up on laws and let your paws
touch the ground
let your beast roam
and sink your talons into me

I won't act too surprised if you're glad
when the moon in me comes out
in the form my eyes can take

looking at you like a benevolent lunatic

when they look deep in you
from inside these wild ones
you'll know–

the ground inside you
will rumble

What Do You Hear When You Listen to Lichen Grow?

Under the spell
of a turbulent creek in a mountain cave
you listen to lichen grow

Under the smell
of a wicked winter rain
you listen to a landscape's
green resurrection

Enchanted, you become velvety
like moss
patient like stone
beflowed like water

and suddenly remember
that you are in fact

a songbird
a spiderweb
a sprouting buckeye

and wild like worms
in the hill beside/inside you
navigating the flood

What do you hear
when you listen to lichen grow?

Wild Syllable of Trust on My Lips

There's absolutely no way
you can be a sun god
if you're not simultaneously a dung beetle.

You are no part-time lover—
there's no way to be one of the great lovers
without claiming your name
from the center of Earth

without pulsating the No-Name
from the center of the moment

the grand pulse hidden
in the Everything

No grand ascent without the dark
and mysterious descent.

No flying without digging.

You are not here to flee from parts of you
you think you can't meet in yourself.

So stand with arms outstretched
and a wild syllable of trust
on your lips

comprehensible only to those
with the great longing
pouring in and out
of their cracked ear hearts.

Kissing Other-Kin In the Center of My Cells

The meaning of "I am because we are" expands exponentially when seen through the lens of deep ecological becoming.

We can start with the stunning, under-appreciated fact that I am more 'not-me' than 'me'—more non-human cells than human cells, by a magnitude of at least ten.

Not the least of these: bacteria and fungi thrive in our gut, without which we'd die. Or microscopic mites having sex on our face at night.

So let's get one thing queer: there is no exclusive 'me' that doesn't include a 'we'.

Kissing microbe kin within me, I am alive.

Additionally, we are mostly H2O. Brains & hearts are 73% water. By molecular count ever higher. Even bones are watery. We are truly water creatures.

Kissing water kin within me, I am alive.

All this is remarkable, worthy of an altar, yet we can zoom in on a single cell. Amidst the plasm (ocean broth) of a cell with all its robust playgrounds are fun little dudes called mitochondria. They kick it by burning and breathing, allowing me to type this & you to read it.

Their ancestry lineage is epic.

Eons ago bacteria were swimming around, until some mutually negotiated contract was struck—this ancient kin became part of nucleic cells, then joined the evolutionary lineage of animal bodies, including our own.

Kissing ancient kin in me, I am alive.

Zoom even further we find the atoms from which it's all built, carbon and oxygen birthed in stars.

Kissing the star kin within me, I am alive.

Like stars, each burning cell breath requires both consumption and self-sacrifice. The quiet fact is that the sighing out requires elements of own's own materiality, exchanging a step forward into life with a graveyard dig.

This eating of ourselves and other bodies to grow more life, this grand metabolism (metabolē = change/throw over"), this death at the core of life—this is the foundational other-kin.

The extent to which we fear this inescapable death, we fear ourselves and Life. When we fear ourselves, we shrink the world and blow pain through other bodies.

But what if we embrace this death in our own depths?

Kissing death-kin within me, I am alive.

Cell-ebrate!

Activating Metabolism, Acquired and Acrobatic

"With my littermates who find a rich wallow in multispecies muddles, I want to make a critical and joyful fuss about these matters." —Donna Haraway

For those not used to eating starlight, this incarnational invitation might seem arcane.

But it's really quite simple: Because we're not yet bioluminescent, and have difficulty doing things like photosynthesizing or reckoning with our ancestral trauma, we both offer deep bows of gratitude to and partner with other-kin to metabolize what otherwise is impossible as so-called individuals or individual species.

This is one aspect of the poly-centric, poly-morphic, multi-generational, multi-dimensional, multi-dementia (out of mind), eco-poetic process we can call the Grand Metabolism. It's the aspect that has the potential to become conscious through the creativity of a creature called 'Homo sapiens sapiens.'

It might even be fun.

We already do this unconsciously (somatically) in many ways—We use gut bacteria/gut bacteria use our bodies to meet certain nutritional needs (vitamin K production/ metabolizing). This mutually beneficial arrangement complicates any notion of separate bodies.

What this inquires into and invites is how we might partner with other bodies who we DIGEST and in-

CORP-orate (move through and make a part of our body), TOUCH (via one of our 53 senses, including proprioception, gravity, temporal, etc), or IMAGINE.

A couple examples of potential INpossible acquired and acrobatic metabolisms:

1)We eat grasshoppers and with the above methods (digestion, touching, imagination), we enter into a relationship of curiosity and further entanglement, finding ourselves empowered with locust-level appetite, able to eat previously indigestible fields of grief, for example, a plague-proportion metabolism.

2)Some Fungi secrete enzymes and oxidants whose superpower is breaking down cell walls (lignin & cellulose). Among other things, this decomposes the forest, making nutrients accessible to the rest of us (whether bacteria or plants or humans).

Quite literally and quite poetically, we all live in the gut of fungi.

What would it mean to enlist fungi's ancient, brainless metabolic wizardry for dismantling the toughest psycho-spiritual walls that form the infrastructure of dominant/dominator culture (to use bell hooks' phrase)?

In activating such acrobatic metabolisms, we not only de-atrophy our muscles of cosmic embodiment, but become co-conspirators of evolution.

P.S. Evoking exotic/erotic enzymes as engines of transmutation focuses on its utility specifically for the purpose of dissolving imperial incarcerations.

P.P.S. Imagination itself is a subtle (or volcanic) form of both magic and metabolism and it's a beast worth a tickle.

P.P.S. Sticking with grasshoppers, we might invite their encoded capacity to hear with ears on their elbow into our own body and imaginal cells, making previously unknown frequencies beyond our specific programming available to us. What might we hear with our extended nervous system (aka embodied consciousness network)?

We Are the Monarch Who Finds A Way

We dreamt we were a dolphin
dying on the shore
stomach swollen with plastic

We are that dolphin

We are the bee with no home
whose family rests
like a lifeless carpet on the ground

We are the 6th Great Extinction

the missing migratory path
the squandered topsoil
the oil in the water
the last of the halibut
the pine tree ravaged by beetles
the mountain gorilla saying goodbye
the Gulf dead zone
the diminishing snowpack
the coral reef bleached by acid in warming seas
the child with asthma poisoned by air

We are the memory of Roughie the tree frog
who kids will never see
the last of his kind

We are the California coast redwood
most of our kin cut down

But our identities shapeshift:

We are also the lizard that regrows its tail
the comeback of the grey whale

the monarch who finds their way
the orangutan that lives another day

We are the seeds planted in prayer
sending songs of hope in the air
for the resurrection of interconnection

We're the ears to hear
the earth's sounds
perennial roots in the ground

We are the Sierra yellow-legged frog
returning against all odds

We are the remediating mushroom
and the artichoke bloom

We are the vacant lot turned to food
the attitude of gratitude

We are the salmon swimming unimpeded
up and down stream
tattooed lines of the earth's dream

When we can't remember who we are:

We see the dandelion
busting through the concrete
and know where wisdom lives

We are the monarch who finds a way.

ACROBATIC EXPERIMENTS IN WETNESS

Your Body and the Bear's Growl

Your body and the bear's growl
tell the truth

Just as there is no arguing
with the spring or elder trees.

Your yawn and yell
your beast and breast bared
the tickle in your dream-yet-dared

are rivers of their own unfolding.

The river song insists and you comply.

The snake's surprising sermons
do not go unheeded.

Damn the censors!

No—Bless them with beauty
your rich revelry raw and rivaled

only by the
Unashamedly Themselves

After all, the censors are only wanting it too.

So compost the joyless judges
in your kingdom of fungi

Retire shame
from the grammar of your unfurling.

If it's too much for them
it's because they've wounded
their own belly
with the blades of poor belonging.

Are the waves offended by the full moon?
The soil aggrieved by the million seeds?

The fruiting cap bashful after the rains?
Does the poppy hide the promise in their petals?

The ancient longings
can't help but burst
the tight shells of humility.

Still, a quarter and a quarter yet
lies asleep in the dirt in us
awaiting the wake up call

that irresistible pull
into the Big Stretch

inviting us to make the music
and the music is all there is

Kiss Me a Blackberry

Do you remember the old sounds?
Are the old tastes still in there?

Let's put our paws up
and funnel them in

all the silent prayers of a pebble
the impossible bursts of Ha!

Do you hear them? Can you taste them?

Abundance spills into all, all plump and play
as waves rave on for days

Teach me water, Sun is here
even in the longest nights

Paint yourself all the early joys
and meet me at the bottom of things

where the doors swing open
Who steps in? Does it wiggle?

Take your shoes off and step through—
we'll caress our shapely wounds

Speak your pain,
the owl has ears

I'll be a Duke of Willows,
you a Queen of Mud.

I want to hear, I want to taste
it all

Kiss me a blackberry, stain your lips
rich with longing

Flow me your inscrutable peach
and dive me silver, whale-deep

for we are no mere ponds to cross
but unfathomable seas

The grand splashes are here
Do you hear them?

Let's put our paws up
and funnel them in.

A Sacred Bee Perhaps

Let's look at desire from another angle—
wide and gentle
pointing this way and that

a Sacred Bee perhaps

all these urgent heart-mouths
of the world

the intos and out-ofs
all the coming-together

or not at all

open to one particular perfect pitch
reassuring hum and dance

buzzing Middle C
or any note at all
releasing seed

hips sway and open
the magnolia blossoms—
sexy citizens of the pollen-nation

water draws up
into the heart of things
and flows back out

bravery is in the receiving All.

Each motion is earnest,
a wet wanting. it wants
to heat things up

and be heated up

like sun warming soil, hot
and handsome seeds are everywhere
kernels of desire

smell it, lend your nose–
all this reaching out
and touching

everything's a finger
a soft gaze
a dance

the length and the shape of a tongue
a vibration
a beautiful beast
abuzz and alive

so tender, so pure—
How can you not be in love
from an angle like that?

Wet

Imagine the curiosity of a raindrop
at the start of their pilgrimage
from inside a dark pregnant cloud

the ecstasy of being alive
and trying on new shapes
as acrobatic
                      experiments
                                                          in

                                    wet-ness

the eagerness of growing down
but also the hidden terror

of

the

free

fall...

uncertain where
they might end up
or what their wet purpose is

Imagine them sharing
in the erotic wrestling of it

Or the play of that sweet surrender
to a trajectory of feeding life

with gratuitous beauty

a soft melody or driven rhythm

Imagine finally arriving
on a distant shore

so different than the house
they were born into

or the path they've been on
their entire life

Only to learn that the destiny
towards which gravity has flung them

is just the launching dock of a new path
among the silent, be-soiled ones

inward into textures so strange
to the touch

it draws them not just close to one other
but inside one another

encountering species of aliveness
about which they've only heard rumors

such wild intimacies with micro-beasts
reaching out in the dark humus of it all—

What a delicious dark thriving
there must be in all this deep wet

What a delicious deep wet
there must be in all this dark thriving

Wild Well of Need Well Met

Mist and rolling
'round each other's moist and swelling
Wrapped around my wrist, her fingers
mine around her neck, enfolding

She's the river wet en-winding
in her arching, aching canyons

I'm the salmon wild, sliding
bold her belly, flesh and flashing
pink and operatic lashings

Gasp! Gripping parts so holy
all the lips and hips so slowly

Begging tongues to dart and dare
daring depth and deeper yet
tasting teasing falling filling
rocking raking sultry sweat

Then floating on the well-sung sheets
having flung so fierce unfaltered
sleep and sweet the deeply-filled
wild well of need well met.

Bryosensual

I wanna stain myself moss green
and make meaning with our skin

like my tongue bepurpled
from blackberries, but

the thickness of winter's blood
is a distance even sunny seagulls can't erase

yet I can't deny it leaves tracks in me
every time we flirt like this

spreading spores and spells
under moons and misty moods

dreaming of tides of touch
and shapeshifting each other's sessile shores.

Oh Nom Nom

It's true, I want to taste
on your tongue the sun
hidden inside the pomegranate seed

to smell on your skin your camaraderie
with wild water

Yes, I'm a bear with paws for persimmon
and your inner pear

full of heat for hip upon hip, yet hope
to touch that holy spark

ruby ripe in darkness
where no eyes live

yet where all true knowing takes place—
This is where I want to meet you.

Where your war and peace slowly cum together
circling 'round the fire

In that altared space let's become beparadised
and speak a language beyond words

devouring each other's everything
like omnivoric lovers—
Oh nom nom and ow oh wow!

Mystery of Red

Oh the mystery of red in the world! The darkest weeks of the year bring the brightest reds.

The same desire that stirs in the rose
to offer herself in deep summer tones
lures firethorn's pomes and scarlet sprays
out for a dance in deep autumn's play

then lands on her lips the color of wine
taking a sip of the season with mine

A touch of the wild conjures the red
to the soft of her skin, pomegranate fed

then rolls in her mouth so ruby and rose
with flickers of tongue like a serpent in pose

so eager to taste, and longing to bite
yearning to sink in the neck of the night

when the seasonal rains finally come
the land and body both are a'hum

when the release of it all finally arrives
all of the daring reds come alive

with the rush of her blood flushing her cheeks
and all of her lips flooding like creeks

beyond their banks in wet wild flow
the land and body alike are aglow

Secret Mandala

Layer by layer the slow unfolding
of a wet and warm truth
known only to the dedicated ones

Like a scholar I read the grand grammar of her skin
with my fingertips
as we caress all the wild things into being

I drape my nose from horizon to horizon
of her scent
across the landscape of her holy hips

across the sunset sighing peach and promise
into the night

My skins on all her skins
around the cupid of her neck
I lace my talons

wrapping my name around her ribs
of surrender

Soft as granite is hard
the face of her inner lips launch me—

I study the hieroglyphs etched
on the mandala between her thighs
the source of magnetic fire—

How untranslatable
how refined the marks
how like the First Spark

My tastebuds string themselves

through the forest
of all her dripping dreams

until she whispers the primordial word
on the lips of a perfect poem
drawing me into her sacred circle

and with my Rosetta Stone
decode the secret song
in the deep of her ancient art
pink with the wet wink
of creation.

Wild Rose Hips

I want to say it's her wild hips

how they move
with the slightest direction

how they hold her flower up

But really, it's how she tastes the world

how she touches it
at every opportunity

how she stops to smell
its everything.

Yes, one could talk about her beauty

how she strikes red and warm
against cold blue winter skies

but really, it's the way she moves
with the wild wind

Yet she isn't merely floating—
she has feet on the ground,
vulnerable and bare

Oh, she has her thorns, trust me—
you can't have one without the other—
and bites real good

The blood's still flowing

But how it was worth it,
and I give my blood back to her
as an offering—

for I, too, am in the world
and want to taste its everything

BEAUTIFUL BEASTS AT THE CROSSROADS

Beautiful Beast at the Crossroads

*"Every step we take on earth
Brings us to a new world
Every foot supported
On a floating bridge*

*Know there is no straight road
No straight road in this world
Only a giant labyrinth
Of intersecting crossroads*

*And steadily our feet.
Keep walking and creating."*

– Federico García Lorca from 'Los puentes colgantes / Floating Bridges'

A beautiful beast at the crossroads.

On the paths that cross or split there's a third that runs vertically or cattywampus through the scene, unseen.

It's *this* that crossroads refers to, regardless of which direction you lend your next step. It's *this* crossroads that threatens/promises to thwart our thoroughfares. Our stale habits and thick theatrics. Our thin theologies.

We tend to leap to meanings before we've even let the encounter *encounter* us. But if we're not careful, Meanings capital M will lock us away from being alchemized.

Ask yourself: If I told you I met this snake person, would you allow it?

I mean eye to eye, soul to soul.

If I told you they slithered in and out of my sacred wound/gift just to conduct research into my integrity, in what pocket do you put that information?

If I said I attended a serpentine seminar into the gift of power/powerlessness, would I get continuing education credits?

Straight in one ear, down my throat into the caverns of my curiosity, coiled up around the bones of my agenda, flickered open a memory or two, and slid out through my belly button.

And that was even before I saw them with my retina.

Catch the light, carry the wind, test the world's ear, rewrite this river—with the blessing and warning of the sidewinding snake with a thousand hearts.

Not delicate, but deluge.

Not going somewhere new but creating somewhere new.

The Deeper We Crawl, The Brighter We Burn

The darker the eyes, the further we see,
slithering down in a slithery spree,
slithering up, slithering free.

In stillness, we flicker the world open
and feel all the vibrations

winding our bodies
across the belly of the earth

slithering out of the old
and into new

powered by that old soul-song
of grandfather serpent
who knew the first rhythms.

The deeper we crawl, the brighter we burn
slithering round with slithery turns,
slithering in our slithery yearn.

Suddenly, I Was a Bear

Crooked trail, glint of sun
wildflowers and that patient breeze—
Suddenly I was a bear.

I knew I was a bear
because when I went to the creek to drink
my hands were paws,
wet with liquid mountain,
sharp in claw.

From a snout distinctly not my own
unfurled a long pink tongue.

But I tell you, the day was warming up
the water tasted fresh
so I lingered as a bear by the creek
sniffing the sundry sun-dried scents on the wind.

I had no names for them.
I had no names for anything,
so I lingered yet more.

If there's such thing as bear-thinking
it's a gigantic knowingness
a granite certainty
a muscular intimacy
with the mountain
and its landscape of aromas
its overflowing and lupine laziness.

Signaling the anchoring of the day
the dark ridge leaned its broad shoulders
into the light.

As my bear awareness shrunk
I could feel a dimming.

I began to retract my claws
pull in my hair
shorten my nose and tail.

And once again I stood as a man
on a crooked trail

with nothing but a current to carry
scents of Sierra duff
wild onion and sweat

and the hint of something ursine
pungent and familiar.

Autumn Otters

This is for our river otter friends on the Baduwa't and Trinity Rivers. And for William Stafford–the poet, not the pirate. A fellow Midwesterner and embedded West Coaster, a quiet of the land, who also inhabited the edges, evoked the nearby faraway, whose 'job it was to find out what the world is trying to be.' He was at home on earth and met the world well.

Otter people are on the hunt
fishing for the best playground

Whatever the day has swept downstream
the otter people accept
with open paws and a keen eye

Even-tailed in the evening
they regard it all with a river's grace

"Here," one says to the other.

"There," the other says,
"over those rocks
around the next bend."

There's always that someone
who wants to peek around
the corner.

But the first scrambles
upon the far bank, whiskering,

"But how could it be better than here
with all the alder leaves

and autumn giving her debut dusk?"

All is negotiation in this life
no different among otter people.

A compromise is reached:

first a dancing on shore
then a slinking back into the silver water
around the next bend

floating like river clouds
whisker-faced and free.

It is a world well-met.

Scribbling Newt Bellies

I found November
just standing there
naked in the forest

but for a thin cloak of mist
clouds in his head
feet in his mud

nothing better to do
than scribble newt bellies
across the land
playing pop the mushroom

dripping dew from his ferny nose
wild syllables from his skin

Sea Lion Soul

If just for a moment
that sealionsoul of yours should swim
(on a whim)

among the great-green-blue-white eyes
of the day
(to play)

and you meet it there
sunning so slick and barking
(larking)

and you bark back
out of respect
and celebration
(in this mammal nation)

recognizing in each other
your animal truth
(in claw and tooth)

you might see proud beings
of sea and earth
(and mirth)

Did you catch a glimpse of a grin?
(yet again)

Thank You, Bear, Devour Me

When bear came to evict me
I was *almost* ready to surrender

I knew there were new worlds
I needed to step inside of

But what I never told you (or any one)
but Grandmother Spruce and the swamp lanterns

hugging the shoulder of the secret creek
that lent me flow

was I'd had an argument with the gods
of love and fate

I'd had an argument with everyone
worthy of standing their ground

when the cold rains thundered
I thundered in return

my most furious curiosity
asking the age-old questions

I made demands, I made myself
a fool, fierce and wet

I knew Bear was coming
for he'd been arriving for some time

In dreams he gave me a spring kiss
on the snout

after a winter warning from the forest edge
I wobbled and froze in fear

He blessed me on the river,
and I stepped inside his fur

teaching me to shapeshift
under summer suns

now, in our home
we stepped into each other's eyes

and I finally surrendered
a fabulous defeat

as we each came out
of a holy hibernation

I'm becoming Bear
and I will be devoured by Bear

at the end of this in-breath
this love-bud, this finger-wide moment called a life

The puncture I gladly accept—
not only accept but celebrate—

For he, this great teacher,
fulfills his purpose

and I won't be found dying
without my purpose punctured

There is no escape—He is wild
and I am drunk on civilization

I accept my glorious annihilation.

DEEP BELONGING

My Name is Belonging

They say the first step
is admitting you have an addiction

So here goes–
my name is Mystery

I've been here
a million times

and Yes, I take heaping spoonfuls of galaxies
when I should be sleeping

I gulp in the seasons whenever I see one
sitting out on the table

My name is Abundance,
and I swallow fat oceans
calorie-dense forests

and whole fields of lupine
when I think no one is looking

My name is Curiosity,
and I look under rocks
climb through dark caves
running my hands
against the wet walls

My name is Insatiable
and I chew
on entire mountain ranges
just to get high

I have no idea what they say
about the second step—

I wasn't listening

I was too busy sitting
on the edge of the cliff
watching Sun retire

and caressing the bark
of Madrone

I was quite occupied
listening to old growth desert
uttering its vast silence

My name is Belonging

Spiral-In-Beauty Way

Let's walk the spiral-in-beauty Way

Let's spin artfully into each other
making a grinlit pact

signed with the wingéd ink
of sunlit trust

Proclaim Yes the shimmers

Proclaim Yes all the hues
of old patterns

of new ripples of love
and all the textures

Yes the great green garments of the season
and its endless faces

But also winter's ancient activism
of turning things under
for a slow embrace

Let's green our hearts
with overtures of awkward gestures

and like plum wine pour the old songs
into each other's laps

until our heart has no more defense
against the miracles

That Which Will Not Be Tamed

Water is the perfect creature
bears are not pets

trees are smarter than us all
and you will never domesticate Wind

They will remain forever wild
like your unquenchable yearn

that draws you into endless topography
of who you truly are—

a beautiful becoming
an evolutionary invitation

relentlessly asking: Can you accept
your gratuitous beauty

as a birthright of being Cosmos
in human form?

Can you simultaneously accept
the radical intimacy and unconquerable distance

between what you love and the heart/heat/home
in the tip of your fingers/tongue/soul?

Called Longing by sacred scholars
it's not meant to be curable

Even when Water drenches you
with their mysterious love

Even when Moon sits in your lap

you want them even closer

If you insist on knowing,
look up on any unblemished winter night

and fling your fancy net
into that sea of stars
who you also will never tame

Perhaps you will catch a few fires
for the hearth of your true home

Arrhythmia

Where did the moon in you go?

To what unworthy machine
have you chained yourself

that even now your heart beats
with such abnormal rhythm?

The hour has come to thrust your chest skyward
to plant your feet and let the season
season you

False beats and terrible tides
and all the big lies have you sweating
all the wrong things

For the dawn and dusk of you
have been hidden too long
behind the purchase of scandalous belongings

Behind the veil of acceptance, a cowardly cloak
woven by strangers' hands

Still, some pulse in you stalks you
the boundless elemental truth in you

pounding out its irrepressible throb
like a whispering lover

who knows your true heart
and its unconquerable rhythm:

Make a dwelling of it

Citizen of Her Flow

This river will be here
long after the country
for which it is named
is lost to time.

It is its own nation—
one for hearts as young
as it is old.

In the headwaters, the pull begins.

It sees the sea and commits.

In the heartwaters, it finds its flow.

It creates a new country
with turns and tides, wides and lows.

In the bellywaters, it takes its fill.

In the soulwaters, it's finally still.

When asked to which country I belong,
I said:

I'm a citizen of her flow.

In This Deep

What could send me down this far
But your wild path bizarre?
Who could bring me down this deep
But your crooked steady stream?

All bowed over and needles fine
Mist and meandering by design
Pitched together in woodly scents
to stitch me in the present tense

Flow and free and green serene
I wondered if you'd seen my dreams
Wet a'whimsied, bewitched between
I wondered if you'd heard my screams

Branched like brooks like roots like lungs
Inside me run your ancient tongues
Your hermit thrush to tuck me in
Then splash of dawn to wake again

Redly barked and mossly packed
I wondered if you'd bring me back
The world's noise had got me good
Until you whispered through my blood

Who could lure me in this deep
But your steadfast summoning?
What could send me down this far
but your wild path bizarre?

All the Way Down

Sling me down, gravity, I won't resist
her labyrinthine turns,
her ups and downs.

I'll take gravity's word for it
and follow her curves down.

All the way down and down further
'cause I'm going for full-bodied texture.

Past her moat, past the dark tower
with its foreboding warnings ringing.

'Cause my ears are tuned
to the beacon beckoning
from the inner chamber

singing delicate rich melodies
the color of a thousand autumns.

In there it's wild and overflowing
like the sands of time, the heart of the sea

Where one might drown
or find a treasure.

I'm going for texture
and a deep belonging.

So yes sling me down, gravity,
I won't resist her labyrinthine turns
and ups and downs.

What I Meant

Meadow mint was meant to lend
its scent to me, was sent to me
as dawnly deer was here to leer
so near to me, so dear to me

and blackly bear had dared
to bare his soul to me,
but not solely he

For You, you aimed to tame
that ol' bear in me,
just barely free

But I yet linger to bring
the wild things to you,
springing through

And long to meet
those wild feet you grew
that true myth in you

All along, I sang the song
of deep belonging,
among the throngs

For I was built to tilt my hilt
at windmills, and not quit until

My heart aroar
and words as swords as skilled as lords,
sing us toward
the secret chords

In That Old Country

In that old country of open air
and littered leaves

we adhere to that traditional way

the one of dirt and dandelions
of wind and winding rivers

conducting those ancient rituals
of walking and listening around the fire

Here, all of us are born
with priestly ears and sacred feet

There is no exile and everyone is seated
at the heart of belonging

We sing the sacred stories
and know gratitude

We migrate, following the seasons
and herds of beasts

across the continent of our souls—
they know where the wild water sings

When the rains come
we drink deeply together

When the sun returns
we wake up

again and again and again

How Many Leaves Have Landed In Me?

How many leaves have landed in me
that I have not yet heard?

That I might shake a cool meaning out of
to launch some secret season

some solemn ceremony
of braver belonging?

That I might compost to build a richer soil?

Might sprout some elegant discourse
wide as sky

thick as the memory of dirt
seasoned with deep time?

How many leaves have landed in me
that I've yet the ears to hear?

ALL THE STONES IN US ARE BIRDS

All the Stones In Us Are Birds

We've left our false belongings
on the shores of a distant city

trading plastic for the eyes of a toad
clocks for purple twilight

Stone knows how to be here
and all the stones in us are birds

Stone fulfills its promise to silence
and all the stones in us are birds

Here, the avenues are all lined with feathers
and the sea's melody adorns us

Do not be alarmed if we become a bird
and nest in your heart

Do not be surprised
if your wings too catch the air

It was meant to be this way, you know—
Everything arrives on time

When we launch at dawn
for high discourse with pelicans

to exchange pebbles and feathers
regard what's left behind

and take care the downy hatchlings
who may need your galactic love—

they have deep longings
that require tending to

Some may want to fly with you
into the storm
making birds of all your stones.

Thrush's Answer

The Thrush's answer ushers in
the last of daylight's questioning

In ever-widening loops he throws
his singsong down, and finally flows

through the finest forest fingers
in my eager ear-heart lingers

Dissolving all the daylong haste
into slow of dusk's embrace

We catch ourselves in melody
no other place we'd rather be

I'm steeped inside his voiced infusion
a moment stopping all confusion

all fret and furrowed brow be gone
no thought of tomorrow's dawn

With each fine measure, each long lilt
I'm stitched into the grandest quilt

He answers all those ancient longings
Pouring out his full-throat woodsongs

Owl

Doesn't need to be seen
but occasionally becomes visible

as an offering.

When one no longer needs to be seen
one becomes the Big Eye.

Vision as gift of the dark,
hoots as forest prayers.

The night is young.

Wild Wings of Mourning

Crooked-neck egret flaps their wings
once for every death it brings

100,000 now in hallowed flight
the Heron hunts in morning light

Crooked-wing harrier sharp in beak
Counts the losses with each shriek

Meadows full of mourning wet
the humans have not met it yet

Swapping solemn slow with haste
Succeeding at ungraceful pace

Rituals of normality
Replace facing mortality

Crooked-croak bullfrog breaks his throat
to sing the songs that grieving wrote

To sing the songs that might be heard
If human hearts could hear the birds

Crooked-neck egret flaps their wings
A prayer for all the precious things.

That Skunk of a Raven

They say as long as it's not a poem
about Nature

or god forbid, Love.

Whether in its burning purity
raw and requited

Or in its complex unrequisitions.

So don't expect nightingales here—
I've turned all my warblers to ravens
and put in an order for dread
or the heavy metals of a world

hell bent on celebrating rank
and shallow things

punching at all the Others
it thinks lives *out there*.

But it boomerangs back
as a dark bird singing sonnets

Summing up the kerneled heart
inside the fist

So I climb down a burnt-out redwood
watered with freedom

seeding its uncompromising truths
in the shade of the season

Shaking out eternities of tunes
from the raven-lit branches:

"The opposite of love isn't hate
but indifference," it says,

"...and there's no room in these wings
for that."

That skunk of a Raven squawks something
about how every tune is a love poem
even the damned curses

How every word, a wild word
and challenges me to defy him.

How can I argue with someone like that?

Bright and Awe-full Symphony of Things

From an ancient spruce
these scratch marks float up

like a black flock
writing sleet-soaked secrets
into the canvas winter sky

Faster than sound, they chirp
a slickening thunder
woven with a frightening light

so close even your cloven bones
run up a lucky tree seeking shelter
called love, fearful

of getting struck.

But it's no use—The tree conspires
with the throat of birds whose wild words
are wrapped in a destiny
in which there is no safety zone.

So you might as well free
your copper raptor
into the moonless night unknown
and soar beside them

You might as well stretch
your thirsty ears on their quenching wings

You might as well lend your glistening feathers
to the bright and awe-full symphony of things.

Show At the Edge of the Meadow

I get dressed up in my Sunday Best
forest tie and obsidian rainbow cloak
to go to the debut show
at the edge of the meadow:

Owl Kills Rabbit

The actors are my brother and sister
I love them in equal measure
both up for Academy Awards
nominated for Best Actor

Meadow's up for Best Set Design—
the production company is well-resourced
and in its millionth season

Opening scene, dusk:

a rabbit munches afternoon snack
suddenly, unbeknownst to bunny
a shadow swings down

The Argument:

knives from killer sky
pierce the jugular, jumping
scream of the bunny, heaving
high-pitch horror, bleeding
body kicking, raining
remains of rabbit quickly
into ancient darkness

Denouement:

Hoots draw the curtain close
on a winter afternoon

Artemis smiles from the east.

A cold silence resumes.

No Longer Here

Those birds that I still hear?

Those birds are no longer here
We've taken all their homes, I fear.

(Feathered songs for which I long
Each day one more gone)

Those stars we no longer see?

They too have disappeared by degrees
behind our screens of light they flee.

(Fire songs, for which I long
Each day one more gone)

Vast silences no longer heard
They've gone with all the birds
Replaced by waves of noise and words

(Quiet songs for which I long
Each day one more gone...
gone).

Did You Grow a New Bird, Forest?

Did you grow a new bird, forest?

Or you bird, did you sprout a new song
throwing spring melodies into the late winter day?

Are you a message from that savior, Change,
or a ringing from my dreaming blood?

Both saying, join
the first bees in their innocent invitation:

Come, play, track
your labyrinthine questions
through the relentless turning of the season

Take the shape of the wind
and alliterate your arriving
with your own alluring lure

PERMISSION

First Permission

At last the hour of celebration arrives
and you step out into that place of first permission

A tidal wave, perhaps
beyond what is deemed right
All signs of warning washed away

Or maybe a mouse before dawn
stealing crumbs,

frogs raucous and rubbing
against the night

Or a seedling gently drawn
by its shameless desire,
your unnamed guest

Because you love the scent of spring
which demands nothing of you
but your own fresh start
and truth-telling

Permitting all the splendid contradictions
aligned with your deepest root
in agreement with the wild things

So now is the time to celebrate,
the clock strikes forever

So bring out the good water
and the glassware adorned with the faces
of all your lucky gods

"Let the permission begin!"

you say with grit and gratitude
in this short and simple prayer.

Catkins Can, Can You?

Catkins can and dare to draw
the early bees with nectar sweet

Scents have sense to sail out
Like dew-drop dreams set to sea

Trigger trigger hie-thee-hither!
Dig thee deeper and never dither!

Planting pollen everywhen—
now and now and even then

Even now, amidst the cold
all destinies and bounty bold

Like shadows, that grow then fold
as hail forms robust and round,
then falls and fades into the ground

All beings inside and around
Stage their plays and subtle sounds

Without a script, but without a doubt
All within and springing out

Yes—All the urging to emerge
As much to show, as converge

And I ask myself,
So I ask you too:

If catkins can
can you?

Trust, Beaver

As empty as a beaver skull—
that's how the big trust is
and as full as the life that got you here.

Not knowing when you'll be in the river
or beside it rotting.

Chew on life with your tremendous teeth
or let it gnaw you to bits–
your choice.

What do you want them to write on your bones?

Password

To where windows are open,
or none at all, withdraw.

Give up on all avoidable walls.

To where fences are figments of imagination
and rainbows more real than nations, scout.

Cast the keys to all kingdoms out.

Let your eyes find gifts more near
the dawn to prick your holy ears

Elude the noisy net and daily cast to catch
the dragonfly duet of your pitched and perfect patch

to where the rhythms hard or soft flood in
imprint them in your luscious blood again

and trace the long-journeyed talking tree
through the four gates of life for free

a delicate dance that can't be seen
without committing to season's scene

Find yourself someday, somehow
on the other side of an audacious vow

the secrets spilled, on display
by every gust and guest of glade

and a cheek against the live oak skin
can tell you the password again

When That Hard Marble Hits You

When that hard marble hits you
from within

Open a nearby window
or dare to walk the shore of night

Pick up a Sitka spruce or a mountain
and set it against the horizon

Let it hover there
'til the sun's removed

See the shape it makes
silhouetted against the moon

Then see what shape your body makes
with your prehensile heart

silhouetted against your sorrow
big like midnight

Make some animal movement
and with guttural grief or gusto

or some unknown, unpartitioned yelp
volley that damn marble towards the distant shore,

the other side of the sea,
some shore you cannot see.

Letting it be known to all, including yourself—
you are alive!

Not Different Than

Don't make the mistake of believing
your unspoken desire is different
than dawn's open hands

or spring's earnest tuliping
trying to escape the dark covers
of winter

Or other than the tide—
sometimes high, sometimes low
yet always showing up

Without it how would
the birds and the shoreline
feed themselves?

How would the world continue to be created?

How would *you* continue to be created?

Don't be fooled into thinking
your red raw art

or sunbow wow
on your face

are different than egret wings
flapping under the crescent moon.

Ok, if you came at it sideways
with a Crab-eye-point-of-view
the portals do look different

They might appear as pockets of mud
waiting for your thirsty feet
even if you bring your shell
far into the day

But certainly don't make the mistake
of thinking your feet are different
than your fathomless heart
deep as the memory of the sea

Cut One From The Mystery

Be no dead dust mote settled
but under-take the old ritual:

Forage from the brambles of time
the forbidden meter of your love

Your elemental kick
soaring and sibylline

Be no dead dust mote settled
but stirred up like a comet

flashing in dark skies
fierce and fearless as

a firenado, world destroying,
world renewing

Pour your roar of ardor
and squawk of frolic

from beyond the melancholic treetop
of your all-baffling brain

From the low hum of nerves
and gods called dreams you misname

Gather what melodies remain
amidst the silence sustained

in that vast field of Mystery-
and put them in your boundless basket.

Caldera: Sacred Well

Sometimes you have to explode
with such a fury
the landscape is utterly rearranged

meaning nothing less
than the end of the world as you know it

If a scream erupts from within saying
'I am not afraid of losing everything!"

You'll know you are on the volcanic edge
of something real

You'll have found that sometimes
you have to fall in upon yourself
to form a magnificent basin

Your job now is to collect water

That's it, that's your whole task for eons–
collect water

so cold and pure
so calm, so cerulean
you become a mirror
for sky creatures and surface-dwellers

Don't worry about where the water
will come from–it will come

Don't worry if you can hold it all–
delegate these tasks to the wind

You're building beauty and the sacred well—
things not to be rushed

When they gaze upon you
they might not see your depths
but they'll feel it

If you meet at all,
you'll meet at the point of mutual depth

some will venture down
to step into you
only to find their own beasts stirring

Keep showing off your brilliant blues
but whatever booms below
keep as a secret treasure

for those daring divers
willing to risk their surface sense

willing to swim new questions
that can only be asked from within
the caldera

willing to risk the danger of drowning
in order to turn the world
towards the sacred well

Madrone Skin

Madrone skin surrenders her skin
bay laurel loses their leaves

cliff crumbles
pollen stolen

spider's gossamer web wasted
without weeping

creek banks erode
gnarled roots exposed

yet what whimper?
what groan?

Leaving the Grass

Though the stalks are dry
though they may have been dead for years

How you, in the tall grass, still hide

Though whatever hunts you–
or you think hunts you–
hunts you there as well

And while you feel safer
among the reeds

you can't see well
nor stretch your legs

Nor cast your astonishing voice
into the wide-net sky

Sky, who needs your songs
to unlock the clouds
and release new rain

So much depends on you
leaving the grass

What Song-Basket Could Contain It All?

What they call love,
I call the wings of a tree
the sand-song of a river beach
multiplied by spring,
divided by day and night.

So why don't I want to resolve
among the 1-4-5-1?

What works works.

What plays plays.

Still I loiter on the 8th fret, fretting
gazing downstream toward
the common chords

where all the meandering noodles
end up in time,

that great pincer.

Umbilical whoosh and porous I,
out of storm fuse and fury
harvest all in-plenitude

to solo note upon note
while this stalking moon
wanes and waxes wise
reciting Heraclitus as her bloody comrade.

Filled, I want to spill the fullness
into the sky and into her heart
despite myself.

What chord could resolve it?

What song-basket could possibly contain it all?

Loyal to Earth

I want my words to be loyal to Earth

a celebration
like the spots on a fawn
prancing through young pine

or a new dawn dancing
past the threshold of night

I want my words to be soft
as a bunny's butt
and feather grass
smooth as the skin of madrone

Yet also, I want them to be hard
as wild walnuts falling in the fall

And tough as granite breaking feet
and ego

As serious as lightning strikes
splitting spruce

Or climate chaos and corona crisis
carrying away the normal
on waves beyond control

I want them as prickly as a yellow jacket
or poison oak,
that'll leave you itching for weeks

Words that wake you up
like the cold splash of a mountain creek
on your morning face

I want them to lead you
gently into the arms of your DreamGiver

But also to startle the rut mind
like a buck launching from the brush

Or a bright red snow plant popping up
among ice cups in the fir forest

an eager invitation
to all of Spring's parties

or a surprise double rainbow
after thunder storms

I want my words
to be stained purple
from picking wild blackberries
and feral plums

Or sexy like a peach rose unfolding
and borage bringing all the bees
to the yard

I want them to allow the wind
to blow through them
like invisible currents
carrying secret scents

tickling the hair on your forearms
that you only notice once it's gone

above all, though, I want them to grow
from the soil, telling the truth,

loyal to Earth

ABOUT THE AUTHOR

Ryan Van Lenning, M.A., is author of *Re-Membering: Poems of Earth and Soul*, *One Bright and Real Caress*, *Trust the Ceremony, F*ck the Ceremony, Trust the Ceremony* and a collection of haiku, *High-Cooing Through the Seasons*. His new collections, *An Ambitious Silence* and *Becoming Beautiful Barbarians* will be released throughout 2025-26. He is the 2019 recipient of Jodi Stutz Poetry Award by Toyon Literary Magazine and his poetry appears in various poetry journals and the book *A Walk with Nature: Poetic Encounters That Nourish the Soul* and *Behind the Mask: 40 Quarantine Poems from Humboldt County*. He facilitates 6-week workshops called Write Your Wild River, Earth Intimacies, and Deep Belonging in the Great Turning a couple times a year.

Ryan is Founder of Wild Nature Heart, supporting people to re-connect with the wisdom of both inner and outer wild nature, to live their callings into the world, and to assist in the work of repairing broken belonging during this Great Turning. He is a teacher, ecotherapist and wilderness rite-of-passage guide and lives among the forests and rivers of Northern California.

ABOUT WILD NATURE HEART

Wild Nature Heart supports people to connect with the wisdom of inner and outer wild nature, to embody our wholeness, and to live our wild purpose into the world in order to inhabit our particular niche in the ecosystem of healing and justice. Through 1-on-1 ecotherapy, earth-rooted mentoring, custom and group wilderness rite-of-passage ceremonies, and various Deep Belonging courses, ecospiritual workshops, and seasonal gatherings, Wild Nature Heart cultivates an ecospirituality that nourishes our deep belonging in the animate web of life in order to do the decolonial work that we are called to do in this moment of the Great Turning.

Wild Nature Heart believes that to cross this threshold into species maturity with a next-season guest pass we must keep our imaginations robust and make moves that subvert inherited paradigms of fear and supremacy. We are being invited to fall through the inherited maps into new territories towards collective liberation. As crises continue to invite us across thresholds of initiation, we crack open the paved highways of our hearts and bodies to allow the tributaries of our holy longings and wild purpose to flow in and out.

The journey is both a daily and life-long practice, as much as it is multi-generational and multi-species. We practice simultaneously being both death doulas to the world that is dying and birth doulas to the one being born.

www.wildnatureheart.com

OTHER TITLES IN THE *RE-MEMBERING* SERIES

The book that began it all:
Re-Membering: Poems of Earth and Soul

The 75 poems in *Re-Membering* are an unabashed celebration of the sensuality of wild nature. Redwoods reach without apology towards the sky, and rivers flow with unflagging energy towards the ocean. This collection re-members Ryan's personal explorations into wild nature, but it also re-collects for all of us a time when our kinship and inter-connectedness with the natural world was self-evident, and invites us to fully re-inhabit and say "Yes!" to our sensual natures, our animal bodies, our playfulness and creativity, connection, mystery, and our instinctive love for this beautiful, sentient Earth.

"Ryan's poetry speaks deeply and clearly to the awakening to our true interconnected nature, which is the only way we can transform our world."
—Molly Young Brown, author of *Coming Back to Life: The Updated Guide to the Work That Reconnects* (co-authored with Joanna Macy)

One Bright and Real Caress

*Build an altar at each moment with a goodbye on the tip of the tongue.
Slow dance drunk in the robust now.
Show up with playful paws and the gravity of worms.
Strap the searchlight around your ribs and shuffle like a crescent moon over all your little resistances.
Saunter past all the gates.
Slit yourself down the middle, pull your skin to the horizon and drip like a mountain.
Can we be here now? Really be here?*

These are some of the invitations lurking in the poems of One Bright and Real Caress. This collection is a celebration of the moment. Of not escaping. Of impermanence. Of death as life partner. With syllables of relentless affirmation, these poems bring an unconditional caress over all the textures of life and our multitudes within. As an invitation to presence and an honoring of the all-too-real struggle to not flee the moment, One Bright and Real Caress welcomes every conceivable crescent mood, slivered and slow, with no aim but to edge out more and more into the whole ceremony and celebration. *One Bright and Real Caress* is Book 2 in the Re-Membering Series.

EXCERPTS FROM RYAN'S UPCOMING BOOKS

From *An Ambitious Silence* (2025)

An Ambitious Silence

What it calls for is an elegant unraveling—
more accurate
and stunning than ever before

sinking into an ambitious silence,
robust and cunning

Do something useful for a change—Listen
so deep and richly
the big ear wants to open through you, remembering
all.

Be unfashionable—
tear the ears off
the false notes.

Shake your feathers
and invite the fox and raven

Until oak reaches into you
and the deep waters gather.

Mud and Moon are your Elders.
You won't get far without them.

Chant Old Man Owl
and Sister Dawn unto you.

That ancient place within beckons.

Unfold it into your bones
and drum your skeletal fragments
until they dance.

Then, like a humble apprentice
pay the tuition for your truth

bartering for the next bold season
with the currency of your heart

letting an unreasonable love
claim you like a throne

and walk your blessed seduction home.

From *Becoming Beautiful Barbarians* (2025)

Off-Script

This is not a dress rehearsal.

This is an undress rehearsal—
We're undressing the stories we've rehearsed
for far too long.

This is not a blockbuster movie.

This is composter cinema—
The only heroes that will be rushing in
are the ones we see naked
in the morning mirror.

And that is more than enough.

With thistles and a raven's beak
we tear up the scripts we inherited.

They are what got us into the Big Trouble.

Liberation is leaking out
of every page of the book
we are writing.

There is no script worth a damn
that doesn't include
the voice of the river
the cries of our ancestors
or the longings living in our bones.

For each mouthful of empty-calorie modernity,
we create a meal of new melodies.
For each megabyte of consumption,

we create a terabyte
of participatory dreaming.

With each breathe we forge
strange and novel toys
in service to the Grand Metabolism.

We are preparing a buffet of the future.

From *Trust the Ceremony, F*ck the Ceremony, Trust the Ceremony*

Door-To-Mystery-Knows-Where

There is a door to Mystery-knows-where
and you are being invited to step through

The new doorway through which you pass
is framed with grander questions

where you'll pick up pieces left
in your canyons long ago

and find on the side
fragments resting by the fire

drinking ale for an evening tale
of dreams wanting to find their flesh

Put them in your wide-brim hat
and home in on your succulent belonging

becoming an obsessionate one
like a convict who loves their fate

This is the door to Mystery-knows-where
and you are being invited through

www.ingramcontent.com/pod-product-compliance
Lightning Source LLC
Chambersburg PA
CBHW071716020426
42333CB00017B/2294